Goodbye Tissues

Also by Deborah Meadows

"The 60's and 70's: from *The Theory of Subjectivity in Moby-Dick"*
    (Tinfish Press, 2003)

Itinerant Men (Krupskaya Press, 2004)

Representing Absence (Green Integer, 2004)

Growing Still (Tinfish Press, 2005)

Thin Gloves (Green Integer, 2006)

The Draped Universe (Belladonna★ Books, 2007)

involutia (Shearsman Books, 2007)

DEBORAH MEADOWS

Goodbye Tissues

Shearsman Books
Exeter

Published in the United Kingdom in 2009 by
Shearsman Books Ltd
58 Velwell Road
Exeter EX4 4LD

www.shearsman.com

ISBN 978-1-84861-013-2

Acknowledgements:
A poem from 'American Possessions' entitled 'far, black lung' was included
in the University of New Orleans post-Katrina anthology *Don Guillermo's
Good Book*, eds. Walter Stone, Jennifer Stewart and Doug Bradburd, edition
of 100.
Segments from this work are in (or forthcoming in) *American Letters and
Commentary*, *Argotist Online* (UK), *Brooklyn Rail: Critical Perspectives on Arts,
Politics, and Culture*, *Fascicle*, *New Review of Literature*, *Tinfish*, *26: A Journal of
Poetry and Poetics*, *Zoland Poetry*.

Cover image, 'Black Watch' copyright © Arkadii Dragomoshchenko, 2009.

Dedicated to Howard

CONTENTS

American Possessions

AMERICAN POSSESSIONS

                    far, black lung
                            knot-spent, gas paltry

decimal, organelle, go?
        convey the stepped day
by horn blast, retinal
                            hinder written or damned
"already"- town.

                    ★

de facto's unintentional hopped-theme

rationality's principle of difference
give over knowledge of singular thing

multiplication's individual
        demonstrael immunity
corpum, lump in the stomack
        sits there, of cause's relation,
elational load, paymaster of intelligible form
        quiddities, camber, the give in *it*,
how imaginary animal runs to type,
phoenix to trait
return's tonical home, old Kentucky or
        sweet's Chicago.

★

after Lance Phillips

speech's speech
       amygdalae's portion *we* sounding—is peanut
wasn't converse hair, place am minimalist

That blowup click to size

Partner's trade one third.

       ★

thus phenosong within interpretation's
limit, wasn't more small nor reverse matter
sub-dancing *were* in terms of stance: here

Question's begin and end, our forehead's rotation

★

Standard's text on *three*
not made of spirit's flesh outwardly
so origin could be first's sensation.

Out there so before science—a master's
service to the word

★

rain's
satiation
of intermediaries,
down-splashing, minds, other forces fail …

Why subtlety's height runs sublime, ends
nourished, western painters, and doctrine.
These mountains' long neighbors, but
is despising earthly things how we teach?

This nations' enemies belong to war. Scripture
where the lowest go, toxic outflow beyond
fruitful bounty

who bindth water from this pool
distills life from poison, an order of sufficiency
to life
whose power.

★

Matter of papers, was say loud
seemingly atmospheric

turning's brain sliced membership—is another
one, too—some, and more

★

Burbled, develop muscle
refined use

so here, *mama*, so right way
was two, high pitch's word

scrim to talk
observed to instinct, against
      run down star
      to naught

      ★

Outdoor shelter let
shed
past
        go as time done

     ★

FATIGUES

the verb of it twelve times off base—
        groups' egg by hour

so homely, blue, watery—

                kitchen counter.

                ★

sourced diphthong's Anglo-Saxon
        right here, hatchet a little
so continuous a rap, knuckled over

                ★

Commercing to recession, upflight's
        angel,
                vacated to point
off-loaded paper swirled
        on whoosh of trucking lane
beyond us
gator-country

                ★

A word's sound, how might trait belong?

Historic bee-buzz, summer cone

    flower
drowse admits a word?
                    depleted, stemless
context

          ★

Not a slow pace,   portational
          parts, applied pads at war
machinic contradiction
          drip oil to lowest rest

inhabited by other's being
field from,   poetational

                    ★

          out in the woods

solemnity's plain black
idea of sumptuary collar

                    ★

Upon (arrow) the phrase . . .

       crop failure's jinx coded shalt-not
shelf for it, others make room in there

       on the wilt, down, drawn back
unhammered soil hardened to pan

       the nothing, bookless loss, calls out
called up, had called down, had called in
       four-ways soral compass on hoof

monitored zone where they grow naturally

       ★

corrected date, kaolin man's cortical image-maker

pretext-lined, crab was elevated

★

firm, affirm yet learn slavery's water
                    strand of sentence
plant life, of *lovely royalty*

symbol in sky fluoresces umbilically
            small child   doubled-singular one
one, right near here
            from around here
animal offspring, a litter
            a school of being
            is being—a Chevy, a priceless
sufficiency how principle of addition
won't lead to deep past, its salt
                            the one indicated

                    ★

            read as counter-symbol
—spring's tree,
thorn, middle
            small paddle-shaped bone
bullet-shattered
from there
                        old lamb's conditioned lunar
light paint-narrowed

                    ★

flower's backbone, drawn
      woven weed   black shall

oven bleeds   shack-wall
      lawn shone flack's bower

drover Leeds' back hall
      brawn one whack's lower

★

long rains   oratorical flourish
managed sector   several of us
word dissociation   tintype

flaked frame of good green doubles

★

Au medial dozing

Who means experts? Steep

crowned take-off, our transport carrier's
length makes pomp of it. A retinue's ransom,
priced proposition either way.

Having struggled over average's
integument
for our topical politic
healstrife, bonebane, reed.

★

against deadening routine's re-arranged
quarters
gaming, tradition's most politic obliterato

ledger reference to maker, initial's price, yet
uncoerced, this sale?

absented from rate's currency:
big city   big job
lone man's kit of necessities?
lodged by force, mosque placement
within diachronic flow, scratched lens.

★

SIMULA STAGE OR ZONE

No reason

for self-selection nor imperfect exercise
of civil rights, an impulse too consolidated.

An urban pathway, a Protestant answer
to catastrophic piercing, wit's sweet delusion,

accommodating one trainee's time, a digital
flight simulator, its crises' rehearsal lubricated

by libidinal imaginings' lieutenant, how pushed
the overriding mentality, a nuts and bolts orientation
automatic at the squeeze repaired.

★

ermine, lumen,
art's body here—synoptics' over-
written word—this blood here-and-now

more than more, what explained

threely, scaffold for writing

★

       their country music—
our home's enantiomorph
our old California court, has a plot

in colonies, workers having stuck together's
meaning sliced and ballad signify

verified haunting, blood-stepped

                    ★

Intended for netted branch,
      hats for truth
                    a very singed frame
still–a field
sophistical
             wire prop for tomato plants in road
             struck undercarriage

       ★

Goodbye Tissues

Portions of this segment derive from various sources including Thomas Aquinas' *Summa Theologiae* in a range from slightly doctored forms of citation to severe disintegration.

Goodbye tissues.

Purity (lens) contains one unit
    and two bottles of solution.

Common sight, however, is understood as neither including
nor excluding subtraction of defect since that would rule
out the possibility of understanding it as in a being which is
sometimes beside existence.

Slim (jewel) case may be the case wherein
space saving abides. As a rewritable pack, you return
to what is there.

Diamond sutra of exempla: if what we directly write are
alleged representations or copies of experiences we never see,
from which we must then infer the experiences copied, we
have no reason to think that the copies *are* copies of anything.

Yet there are no writings at all, only illusory mental states that
compose minds.

A case of dianoia.

Dimensions of filter say "so long" for now.
Here, our basket holds short notes.

For example, *body* is defined as constituent of flavor and
accent. However, because proper principles of accidents
are not always manifest, sometimes we take the differences
of accidents from their effects, such as dispersion or
concentration produces differences of colour, insofar as there
is an abundance or paucity of light, from which the different
species of colour are caused.

Take it black. Amen.

Time, a sustained release, yet our incised tablet
won't last a day.
Can supplement-facts truly supplement
what is theoretical?

Is another doctrine necessary? But any doctrine must be of
existing things, since there is no science of non-being. There
are many supplements to the practice of series in literature,
nature, mathematics, and theology.

All fiction is formed of language.

A thing should be repaired by the one who made it; one
should reconcile oneself to all things.

Tents and watered gardens
near rivers.

Thank-you line.
Blank but secure.

If you do not clearly see the words
"original document" or the security weave
pattern is absent, do not honor this.

Moreover, practical science is concerned only with what is of our doing. But this doctrine includes angels and other creatures which are not work of ours. Therefore, it is not speculative but practical.

Moreover, every science proceeds from principles known of themselves which are obvious to all. But this science begins with believable things, which are not granted by all. Therefore, it is not a science.

Thus perspective, which is concerned with the visual line, is subalternated to geometry from which it presupposes truths proved of the line as line.

                              No inks, perfumes, or lotions
                                    soft fiber on the outside
                                    strong inside
                         one
                         one
                         one
for every good-bye reason,
a good-bye sign.

Widely differing sciences ought not to share the same mode.
But poetry, which contains the least truth, is far different from
the science which is most true. Therefore, since the former
proceeds by way of metaphorical locutions, the mode of this
science should be different.

Poetic knowledge is of things which on account of a defect of
truth cannot be grasped by reason and that is why reason must
be seduced by certain likenesses . . .

cartouche of tint
can it be the only continental mark, yet
     four imprint ideas . . .

recessional field, sunflowers
are they shopped or candid?
     color dot right where you can tell.
                  Right off,
        we can be adjusted by sensor
        coordinated to setting.

Shadows are not something. Matter must be imagined in the
moved thing. Therefore things that share in some motion
seem to agree in matter.

Things that have the same potency have the same matter,
because just as form is act, so matter is potency.

Of geothermal site, its measure.
. . . toucans and parrots stay high;
why depart canopy—
a panther below, a snake, ant, mice.

Swivel eye in blue patch,
the work of six days.

Afterwards the stars were made. My father works, and I work.

Day signifies a certain time; but in the formation of things,
according to Augustine, there was no succession of time.
Therefore he does not retain the distinction of days.

★

"We take for granted that there is a direction to the way
things unfold in time. Eggs break, but they don't unbreak;
candles melt, but they don't unmelt; memories are of the past,
never of the future; people age, but they don't unage."

from *The Fabric of the Cosmos* by Brian Greene

★

things unfold, and they fold
tissue
crease, wrinkle; smooth, plump

AQUINAS: *DIVISION TEXTUS*

Aquinas

two of three tractates where
we find *consolation*

one

three   two

close analysis of the text
(division textus)

afterword
questions

The Exposition of Boethius'
On the Trinity

                      whether the human mind
                            bodily eye
            ourselves
            through
                it
                      look ate man
        as the his
            to the illumination truth
        blank sufficient in us, unable

                        ★

(various procedures, constraints, &
defacements of Boethius'
Consolation of Philosophy   mind need mind
                          truth does.
               stated "Not perception
                    mind, lean, those learn,

Article 1: Does the human mind need
a new illumination of divine light for
knowledge of the truth?   unless Teacher can eye
                          as
                          by
                        then
              light to be but labour

                        ★

light to be but labour
    twofold second
    the first
    light for
    of God

it is—one, does
knowledge of—first question
light in   it seems
2 Corinthians   '. . . think anything . . .'
Therefore, the   illustrated anew

it is   it on
to those,   learn from
say in   thirty point three
is illumined as the
intelligible things
eye can the material
it, is, acts are
for their   three-are

★

third in alternates

so, therefore we   within us principles
we must be   truth in order
operation of the   human mind is

light than the   of lower sensible
have forms which   principles of natural
cannot bring off   the stars on

increases them, therefore   neither does the
as it were   human mind to
light namely the   supervenes the same

causes are ordered
and not *per*

first cause

★

.

——mind is sealed therefore requires another
    ——finished with by can
just activity within agent need know
                is
matter bodily suffices all artifacts of
        like some——

                ★

"e"

be difference between active passive powers
the passive powers perform their proper
operations unless they are moved active:
sense sense unless

"a"

active can operate
as vegetative
realm are am active, namely agent
and a passive

"i"

possible intellect is intellect is
this is opinion Avicenna
which is in its
operation which is it is illuminated

"o"

outside of
words of Philosopher *On Soul* to
power of soul, something harmony
authority of professes

                           "u"

———

thus soul
truth
just natural

            "a" "e" "i" "o" "u"

a, any, Hence, it, to, such

        ★

after Hölderlin

Article 3: Is God the first thing
known by the mind?

   Against thought held by
dreaming snakes
   we judge what we know
as first-light necessary to sight, so
we might have *things* in light.
   First, the sky swivels from
a pinhole held to cathedral spires
   where rain falls on intelligible
things, perception a still life
from which human perception
is stenciled—second to
eclipsed presence.

Why might planed wood
show creation extracted from
raw scenes, set primacy?

   But no, first or last, our boat
let to cradle-rock on perceptible waves
—how we live, each after sight of the face.

★

FURTHER ARTICLES

Article 4: Is the human mind sufficient
of itself to reach knowledge of the
divine Trinity?

"mode, species, order"

Funny, how we can see
a creature and not know
what it is. In the sky and forests and
              seas and theology.

Stars magnify everything.

The creator and its mind: two.

We trace to makers, a word.

Sharing gives us joy.

Fragments proceed from whole.

We might think of what precedes
inequality as prior equality.

Three is perfect.

Mode
species
order.

★

On the contrary:

three=one

satisfied animals are solitary

three days of sacrifice

looked to unknown effect

when a word doesn't link the two

not all arguments are exhausted here

we note distinctive circles

even if distinctions are taken away,
        joy remains

little bodies, celestial bodies

meaning of equality; causes of plurality

a number as a form of completion

many can be *one* here

known in its relations to other things

★

ANGELIC KNOWLEDGE OF IMMATERIAL THINGS

Article: Can the angel by
his natural powers know God?

         … that the country took to dance.

Creature not absorbent.

     Concocted under adverse conditions:
a blade,
        high, bird-carved.

    Brought to white cube,
matchstick, language braid,
bent horn's square dance,
         shuffled text.

Close breath, reserved

base four, flageolet, motility

     over

   ★

On Goodness in General

Article 1: Do good and being differ in reality?

The striped green awning of dollar stores.

Parrots' complaint this morning.

China said to buy up their daily fare.

No correspondence to autobiography.

Mexico begins maybe three hours from here.

★

Most made things, of artifice.

Things salted with a sense of time
that is not metaphysical.

Striped, serial items, re-prints I couldn't
            manage to imply, or was implying.

★

★

With a damaged fuselage, another
show of approbation.

★

Article 3: Is every being good?

added, plankton, planksheer
    contracted skin, fell-kin

resuscitate, hauberk, throw?

   relay arrow's deck
by sawbuck, Esquimaux
    virtue, a drift or prime
flaw-trench, mere nurture.

    ★

near, scenes brachiate
prefrontal's Flemish peasant—arm
wasn't flipper, body

protected unpalatable's drop
lay between
rounds' determined range—

★

explanatory weight: cephalic
lobe in colony, canopy.

★

Article 6: Is good fittingly distinguished
into honourable, useful and pleasant?

motion toward which it tends

★

Four

Sonnets' Four Seasons

Here's a stretcher. A dead dove,

lees pressed into cakes
for lack of meat

pantomime of symmetry, a hymnal

take in dross, exit signs, scratched
        initials of love

                    ★

"after a little combing
and the max ration
there were no abstentions
from darkness to darkness . . ."

from *Eternal Sections* by Tom Raworth

".. . to assert a normal hum
until, that is, the
great big cork tag
of the jury's verdict
rows of boxes
watching many famous figures"

from *Eternal Sections* by Tom Raworth

                         either ingenious or
wrong.

                         opuscule
was miniscule

turned to lesser oracle, neither
infallible nor authoritative

                         corpuscle
              leukocyte, your encapsulated
ending of a secondary nerve

          Vegas, called back
          little line, twilit

                    ★

                              used in ceramics
in response to acidic
                    conditions

                              niritic
hauled up, and as common
to study
in stacks

whaa, whaa, whaa, trombone
          hand-off to comedic dash

withholding treatment,
          national depiction *dies*

                    ★

★

         part martyr
where linger came

        they say   . . . clemency of oaks
as if there were

        not possible to lever words
with more

        yet what we do, marled
thing loves *its weight*

★★★

1.

By section, we're bound to realism,
assures us light necessary, breath may
lead to project and provisional set,
outsized authorial negations or
umbrage at lack of indictment, build is
by state. Here, erased ledger-reference,
our myth with metonymy: folding lamp,
the swerve in pollen's Brownian descent
"bee" applied for, procedural text can
not without blueprint, refined intention,
précis: its honey setting. And today
its copied *build*, body, array marked
more shutters and paralysis echo
toward parity, fourteen lines, more or less.

2.

Render a proof, engulf the war or
use of images (presence) to suggest
residue and residual salt, air-
open as the times require—thus people,
one burning issue to rally around.
On the Potomac persists a marble
national axiom at a hill's height,
theological view of pollution,
evaporation of memory. Our
port egress vigorously marked off or
submit to *nothing*, select against "their"
irrational fear. Deliberately
duet in artistic farce derived from
exploitive *intelligence* as it's called.

3.

They see rows of Renaissance plays. Second
projected onto spring rains, where poor food
smells provide a third stage, make dust and heat
"de-anchored from place"; never mind we can.
Voices fill the theatre: their faces shine.
This is not at the farthest remove from
a laugh nor from Ezekiel's prophesy
but tilted outward, our non-celestial plane.
Of three stages: the bed and pillows are
not had at the train station, electric
sensations abstracted to principles—
go sense the same eternal smell anytime.
An unethical practice to save lives?
Our vanishing point recession:
                            state house to tiny dot.

4.

A dragon assembles a bride-machine.
Middle-period know-how slides to form,
loose study to specialty amplified
at first hint of dragon. Our knight opened
an explanatory parenthesis.
Open parentheses create suspense
that Hegelian dialectics won't
satisfy. A preface may signal troop
deployment, yet the most quotable are
withdrawals from Tikrit that offer three or
more branching paths, a crystalline organ.
Too often, travelers use trees when they
enter a clearing. The knight replicates
item, meaning turned a hazard ground.

5.

for Jacques Roubard
His memory of research in metrics,
anticipations in the 70s
acquiring books to mail home. The fall, rather
temporarily in another country,
kinged by flaw. In lone innocence if he'd
blank surface whereon to trace idiolects
later: unwilled amnesias, draft, or notebook.
So long to get over the king's body.
Lever-like, the early modern mind used
to pry free. Free thought from Thames river, sign,
bloodline. Situated in lineated
space, intact boundaries of nation cede.
Deprive the single-cell organelle
liminality, the future body?

6.

The pilgrim had a moment of truth. Had
of winter, could dispatch both models
make double atomic diagrams clear
to retro-seraphim in humility,
drafted "About torture" and we behold
of written word near material for
allegorical cistern drawn down, or
shifted from spirit to flesh with onset
& copy, yank the derivative land,
yet metaphorical: see, cherubim
wait for whatever as lovely poems are
proto-truths held in common; authority,
comedy. They wept. For bread and meat, our
new lows, a literary spoof falls free.

7.

The secretary assigned a machine
precarious sentences. The body
pays off ratcheting down from syntactic
bolts, each a left-handed thread of Charles River
in that machine. So's I tell ya': four-eyed
to copy down organic political
vines torn from poverty. No gentle
criminality, its features. Myself
-like role recoded the novelist's long,
fully aware of coercion, not
system-assured one pair of sovereignty. Forced
analogies, pity the subversive!
Persuasion swallows these abstractions. More
am nation. Bar dubious election.

8.

Freud compiled stories of long influence;
subjectivities are wracking private
broad human consequence. But more, this call
for your set, the specific nature of
new widows, former residents of burned
long days fashioned by five untenable
testings now disallowed by another
space of stairway, swoop of analyses.
For mediums, rehearsed fantasies, puppet
capitalists bear returns occluding
cities. If the uncanny may reserve
attitudes—of fear, what more can be said?
Nation, our item today during these
shells beyond infantile sensation shall not.

9.

A praedella on Protestant speech act.
Discourse eras can be exemplified
by: Who can these men be?
            Who are these guys?
Tied to mechanized evidence, image,
how concerns about midterm elections
shape Republican message on withdrawn
troops in Brussels. At first, they didn't like
discourse twined in compound, read. On white walls.
Book chained to podium—this depiction
against acts. Recently liberated
"I"—to you, what can be the Fourth of July?
For ease of retrieval resembles game
without residents at rolled, blueprint phase,
has it twenty-four parts or forty-eight?

10.

The speech-writer changes position. Noted
for a prompting "On evil," a moral
term helped the president gain favor. Boiled
the syrup until, against the wooden
spoon, a viscous wave showed transformation
to cold solid. The many vanishings
of the subject. Yet, footprints of a "been,"
or a "was," photographed here, a lab slide,
tissue sample. The sonnet's rhythm makes
our effigy burn bright. The "go-away"
chant of bright vultures double-click with "here
you are," "there you go." Corpuscle ending
to a secondary nerve. Vegas, called
back, so one promise made good on right here.

11.

Not all hypotheses are utopian
as well as logical. Nation within
reservation. General Electric
state, their nuclear waste. How Argonauts
sometimes are the expense of the mother's:
nine plus nine plus one years I've lived right here.
Just blank out lines, reinscribe time so we're
a proposed case that could be disastrous.
This nation exercised rights, made laws as
their herd of blind deer in western New York
held a hard position against the banned
life. "I" am leaving for another place.
Language is lastly forgotten. Sonnets
now pose: what brave new world is for sale now?

12.

Our medium is language not belief.
Space operas exhaust old Roman-
controlled FCC, what airwaves can't,
pirate stations will, subject matter, not new
expense of what dies. Hamas held their guy,
taken out, bombed. Sequence, reliable.
Computerized wandering, replications
of Odysseyian protocols in today's
Catholicism now fed on GOP,
"here for" a well-informed public. Yet
our old epics? What grows will grow at the
sum in retaliation, bridges were
defense against the vase of symmetry,
of self, brush the hyphen, its sectioned plane.

Goodbye Tissues

Portions of this segment derive from various sources including Thomas Aquinas' *Summa Theologiae* in a range from slightly doctored forms of citation to severe disintegration.

14 LINES

Am free
or sticks
safe as content
under pressure.
Stones deplete
youth, layer
remove inches
from surface
on surface,
cloth shield,
an excellent
gas, exposure
means active
verb, induce.

★

natural bodies
imply order
of time insofar
as form
is knowable
alone, as wood
is to bed
part of its essence
acquires another,
other, to the body's
prime implies
time, preceded
disposition, or something
between them.

★

POSITIONS

Quarried, roughly paved, neither autonomous
nor pattern-free, in traffic sanctioned
here, this side of warm currents feed.

★

REMAINDERS

Tomorrow the corporal will correct
the lens then align the frame.

★

The house skeptic
        wiped beads from the bar

said, what more can be
known of the nature of limits.

★

Corporal resorts to tradition
to paper over inventive remarks

when lower ranking stiffs see red.

★

Before implications of the meeting
are fully taken in, the house

skeptic and corporal could only have made
this meeting were time-travel a possibility

wherein the house skeptic exits
the metal platform to a bookless paradise
armed with plain provisions
in sealed containers.

★

POSITIONS

       Mark, secondarily, structures beneath
measure,
       Turn, primarily, oscillations' suspended
plain,
       Resist, as tertiary position, position of rigour
that obtains,

       Precipitate, next, clouds above
engines,
       Emplant, first, gridlines on fixed
gaseous ject,
       Surrender, syllogistically, ordered origin
that determines,

     ★

                              of vessel tendency, lobes
express basis for scale, color, structure
                  figural: old motion-studies, latches,
discourse of articulated bodies, one-by-one,
x-ray style
            economy of cartoon preliminary
to full work; hemistich toward rattle,
relief dissolved, rained on limestone.

                              ★

                        Memoristics, as a capacity.
pebble-shift, flashed-or-dipped plating,
electrosensing or a sort of neural gate array,
                    stringentastringent, sour
invariance dulls us

                    All-over wordwall juvenilia
non-ventral pretense to equivalence
of twenty-first century land-use limits

                    Periodic coloration, as a reference.
legal-splitter, pulsatory circulation ebb line,
                    dispersants found as catalyst role
or twined-apartagents, reduced information
in suffociant ratio to experiencespread.
        suffocate
        sufficiante

                    /space exploration

                        ★

Coda

CODA

after Celan

Good-bye.
Good-bye, Good-bye.
Marked by place,
star-set, word—
go to rest, our result.

Go to rest, our result.

Was, was
truth. How did we
get over—get over
with these words?

Speckled,
Speckled and leonine. Blade-
shaped sort -wort, constellate,
shallow-rooted

it did not take more than
we had, it made a show of
itself, a show
raised us up

       it repaired
the skin of our place
and figured water,

figured
figured water—then

a bird, a training bird
swung from a string
rocks a shadow uphill,
a shadow uphill,
no shadow
for the learned came in.

★

made, made
up,

We wanted to be taken in,
to take in.
Our natural parts
were always there,
and it obliged.

Obliged us, obliged
our fabric, and cleared
each cell, then

no film to cover
those fixed in place, would pond.

Cover and fixed in place

Let in, let on
that portion, fabric
cut to clothe.

Island and capital
made over.

★

www.ingramcontent.com/pod-product-compliance
Lightning Source LLC
Chambersburg PA
CBHW022200080426

42734CB00006B/514